And So It Goes

And So It Goes

George F. Walker

Talonbooks

Copyright © 2010 George F. Walker

Talonbooks
P.O. Box 2076, Vancouver, British Columbia, Canada V6B 3S3
www.talonbooks.com

Typeset in New Baskerville and printed and bound in Canada.
Printed on 100% post-consumer recycled paper.

First Printing: 2010

The publisher gratefully acknowledges the financial support of the Canada Council for the Arts; the Government of Canada through the Book Publishing Industry Development Program; and the Province of British Columbia through the British Columbia Arts Council and the Book Publishing Tax Credit for our publishing activities.

No part of this book, covered by the copyright hereon, may be reproduced or used in any form or by any means—graphic, electronic or mechanical—without prior permission of the publisher, except for excerpts in a review. Any request for photocopying of any part of this book shall be directed in writing to Access Copyright (The Canadian Copyright Licensing Agency), 1 Yonge Street, Suite 800, Toronto, Ontario, Canada M5E 1E5; tel.: (416) 868-1620; fax: (416) 868-1621.

Rights to produce *And So It Goes*, in whole or in part, in any medium by any group, amateur or professional, are retained by the author. Interested persons are requested to contact his agent: Rena Zimmerman, Great North Artists Management, Inc., 350 Dupont St., Toronto, Ontario M5R 1V9; Tel.: (416) 925-2051.

Library and Archives Canada Cataloguing in Publication

Walker, George F., 1947–
    And so it goes / George F. Walker.

A play.
ISBN 978-0-88922-654-8

    I. Title.

PS8595.A557A86 2010   C812'.54   C2010-904429-0

And So It Goes was first produced on January 30, 2010 by Factory Theatre in Toronto with the following cast and crew:

GWEN: Martha Burns
NED: Peter Donaldson
VONNEGUT: Jerry Franken
KAREN: Jenny Young

Directed by George F. Walker
Assistant Director: Courtney Walker
Set and Costume Designer: Shawn Kerwin
Lighting Designer: Rebecca Picherack
Composer and Sound Designer: John Roby
Stage Manager: Joanna Barrotta
Apprentice Stage Manager: Heather Thompson
Production Manager: Aaron Kelly
Technical Director: Jamie Monteiro
Head of Wardrobe: Raegan Moore
Head of Props: Anna Treusch

Introduction

It's dark and I'm afraid.   —Karen, *And So it Goes*

> Many people need desperately to receive this message: "I feel and think much as you do, care about many of the things you care about, although most people do not care about them. You are not alone."   —Kurt Vonnegut

"I'm scared." Standing at a window, looking out into the darkness, the first words of *And So it Goes* spoken by Karen— a young woman suffering from schizophrenia—could very easily encapsulate the entire ethos of the play. And the ethos of the play is one that acknowledges that like Karen, we're all scared, and probably should be, given what's going on in the world (the total ruination of the world economy by a small number of elites, epidemic levels of poverty and violence, the irreversible degradation of the planet, the list goes on …). But despite these worries, and this fear, *And So it Goes* is not a play about big issues. It is a play about a family, a family barely hanging on after their stable existence is thrown into turmoil when Ned ("a husband, a father") loses his job as a financial advisor. Their car is repossessed, they lose their house, and all the while Gwen ("a wife, a mother") is trying to cope with their daughter Karen's disease.

In his previous work the playwright has often given voice to those members of our society we rarely have an opportunity to hear from. *And So it Goes* is no exception. Those who suffer from mental illness are one of the most marginalized groups in our society, but the writer gives Karen a voice (and a formidable one at that) and forces us to listen to it. Karen is trapped in a justice system that doesn't know how to deal with her, and her monologue from the prisoner's dock after she assaults a social worker shows us how ill equipped those around her are to cope with her disease. This has devastating results for her family, and more tragically, for herself.

The role of Karen is a significant challenge for any actor—to explore what it might be like inside the schizophrenic mind and how that plays out in the body while also finding something grounded to connect to. During rehearsals for the premiere production in Toronto, watching Jenny Young discover and develop this character was a deeply engaging experience. While this character's disease is by no means the only aspect of her humanity that we encounter, it is a huge part of not only her character but the substance of the play.

What this meant for Jenny Young (and will mean for any other actor playing Karen) was that her voice, her physical world, and the way she interacts with others were all things that she had to find with the reality of Karen's disease in mind. How far should this go? Does it pervade her every interaction, or do certain experiences and people trigger it? This also affected the choices of the other actors, particularly Martha Burns and Peter Donaldson, who played Gwen and Ned. What are their individual relationships with her and her disease? Do these different relationships with her affect their relationships with each other?

When Gwen asks Vonnegut to explain to her what living inside Karen's mind might be like we get an answer that is both heartbreaking and frightening, but also fully acknowledges how powerful a mind that is unhinged and therefore completely unedited can be.

> So what was going on in Karen's ravaged brain? A lot obviously. Fractured pictures and sounds and fragments and sometimes wholly formed ideas and arguments that passed like sandstorms through her head and then sometimes returned and played out in reverse. Things that were understood from her past were involuntarily replayed in revision while almost simultaneously the world around her screamed for her very critical attention. And she felt things, did she ever. Everything was important, potentially dangerous for sure, but also intensely ironic and inevitable ... everything and everyone ... you and Ned, for example.

In *And So it Goes* Karen's illness is devastating, yes, but it is also a means through which we learn things about the characters that would otherwise be left unexplored. Karen can and does say anything—much of it hurtful—to her parents, and while what she believes to be true is necessarily unreliable, more often than not what she is saying contains within it an essential kernel of truth about the characters and their relationships. At the beginning of the play she tells her father that he scares her, and while in the moment we cannot understand where this fear is coming from, as the play progresses and we learn about Karen and the way her mind works, it starts to make sense. The play also provides us with an opportunity to see Karen healthy, a choice that is important for the play but is also very significant for the audience. Many people who attended the premiere production at Factory Theatre in Toronto suffered from schizophrenia themselves or had someone in their lives who did.

We heard time and time again how important it was to see Karen healthy, to understand how quickly the illness came over her and how in so many ways the sick person simply wasn't her.

Bad things happen to this family though, beyond Karen's illness, beyond the loss of Ned's job. In other of this writer's plays every moment would be spent trying to keep these horrible events from occurring. (Think of R.J. and Denise trying so desperately to gain back custody of their daughter in *Problem Child*.) But in *And So It Goes* it ALL happens, and it seems inevitable. Gwen and Ned are left to deal with what is left of their lives but not without some help from Vonnegut ("a writer").

Kurt Vonnegut is the American master of not only satire, but a humanistic world view that somehow synthesizes the horrible tragedy of the world with an unrelenting comic overlay that makes us feel okay about it. He is perfectly at home in this play, trying to help Ned and Gwen understand the many bad things that are happening to them. Vonnegut is, of course, dead, a fact acknowledged by both Vonnegut himself and Ned and Gwen, bringing an element of the fantastic and the absurd to the play. While Gwen and Ned conjure up their own Vonneguts to cope with the increasing bleakness of their existence, his presence is by no means an escape. He asks them questions they do not ask of themselves or each other and if anything he is a constant reminder that "things could all get so bad you won't even recognize where you are. It won't seem like the same planet." He says this not to be cruel, but rather as a (somewhat stark) reminder of their reality and also of their capabilities to cope with that reality.

While Vonnegut adds a level of the absurd and something verging on magic realism, the relationships and politics within the family are at the emotional centre of the play. At the beginning of the play the nature of Ned and Gwen's marriage seems familiar. A woman knee-deep in the often traumatic realities of family life and a man who is either benignly clueless or potentially harmful. Gwen has been staying home looking after Karen and thinks it is Ned's turn to do the same. Ned on the other hand thinks he's more effective restarting his career, a notion that seems virtually impossible. But all this becomes immaterial when the worst thing imaginable happens to Karen and they are forced to deal with the devastation of their family as they tumble farther and farther away from the middle-class existence they seem to have taken for granted.

Ned and Gwen's journey through the play is both surprising and devastating. The play was initially written without an intermission, but about three quarters through the rehearsal process it was decided to put one in because "the audience cannot handle this whole play without a break." And throughout the run of the play we discovered this observation to be completely accurate. By the time the play reaches the point at which the intermission was added, the devastation of the family seems so total and so complete that audiences do not know how to react. They don't know if they should laugh (for parts are hilarious) or if they should cry (for parts are horrific and heartbreaking.) The intermission gives the audience a much-needed break to process what they have so viscerally experienced in the first act, and when they arrive back in their seats and discover in the first scene of the second act that Karen is not gone completely from the play, the relief is palpable.

Relief also starts to set in when the audience realizes that despite Ned and Gwen's physical circumstances, they are psychically and emotionally moving towards somewhere more outward looking, somewhere *bigger*. As Ned says, standing on a street corner adorned with a sign that says "HOMELESS. OUT OF WORK. AND FUCKED UP," he feels "engaged" with the world in a way he never has before. He doesn't feel better, but he feels in sync. His daughter is still gone and he and Gwen are still homeless, but he feels connected with how horrible and horribly complicated things are in the world, and in so many ways this is better than the way he was before which was exactly the opposite, disconnected and blindly satisfied. As Ned becomes more liberated he also becomes more focused on the aspects of existence that so infuriate him. His appearance onstage wearing his "BIG BLOWOUT" sign is so shockingly absurd that it takes a moment to realize that what we're listening to is not the demented rant of a man on the edge but rather a very impassioned and logical expression of an intense frustration with the way our society works, and more specifically what we need to make our lives okay again. Ned has contempt for the stuff he's hawking, but he knows that we should all just "buy something to keep it all moving along." He's intensely realistic but his vision of how he would like things to be is completely utopian—a disappointed optimist, perhaps. As his energy becomes focused on what happened to Karen, his dark instinct to seek revenge for her murder mingles with his desire to rid the world of dangerous people and make it a better place. While frightening and somewhat extreme, his desperation is understandable. And as we watch him teeter on the edge of a very steep precipice we also witness Gwen begin to teeter precariously on the edge of reality. While Ned becomes more connected to reality, Gwen spends more and more of her time talking to people who aren't really there. Spending most of her day on her shelter cot guarding shoes, Gwen disconnects from everything other than her immediate reality in order to survive what is happening to her. Unlike Ned, looking outward doesn't help. Instead she finds comfort in the details, in the interior and the personal. In talking to Vonnegut and a version of Karen she never got to experience in real life, Gwen creates her own reality in order to cope, just as Ned fastens onto an approach that allows him to feel actively engaged.

And yet somehow Ned steps back from the precipice and Gwen (mostly with the help of Vonnegut and Karen) returns to reality. They are reunited on a vastly different plane than the one they existed on before, and they have found a way to move forward together. The end of the play is surprisingly optimistic (given what we've seen them go through) yet feels right and honest. Things are not suddenly all better for Ned and Gwen when the lights go down for the last time, but we are left with a sense that they—and we by extension—can and probably will be able to survive. We feel reassured.

—Courtney Jane Walker

People:

KAREN: *25, a daughter*
NED: *a father, a husband*
GWEN: *a mother, a wife*
VONNEGUT: *a writer*

Setting:

Various places. No doors, walls or windows. Just lighting. Some furniture. And a soundscape.

Scene 1

Night in the living room. KAREN is looking out the window. NED is reading a newspaper.

KAREN
    I'm scared.

    NED flips a page.

KAREN
    Did you hear me? I'm scared.

NED
    (*looking up*) Get away from the window.

KAREN
    I wanna watch. I can watch if I want.

NED
    (*shrugs*) You said you were scared.

KAREN
    Lots of things scare me, I still watch them. You scare me, I watch you all the time.

NED
    I don't scare you.

KAREN
    Sure you do. You scare the shit out of me. You always have.

NED

> You know, you hurt my feelings when you say things like that, Karen.

KAREN

> Like that's the issue. Your feelings. I'm talking about being scared, and you—oh look, he's rocking.

NED

> What?

KAREN

> He's rocking on his heels. That's so fucking cocky. Why doesn't he just steal the car? If he's going to do it, you know ... just do it. Don't stand there rocking on your heels like you're some super cool big fucking shit.

> *NED stands. Moves to her side, looks out the window.*

NED

> What is it about that man that makes you think he's going to steal our car?

KAREN

> Okay I don't like your tone of voice. Did I ask you to come over here and get involved? "What is it about that man" etcetera ...

NED

> You said you were scared ... then you started talking about him stealing our car ...

KAREN

> Which is what I think. You think something different just state your opinion. I'm open to another point of view on the subject ...

NED
>He's just standing there. Why can't he just stand there.

KAREN
>So that's all you have to say about it? If he steals our car, what will you say then? "We don't have a car now."

NED
>Karen ...

KAREN
>"We don't have a car now. I can't drive you back home."

NED
>Look let's just move away from the window. Let's do the crossword.

KAREN
>I don't want to do the crossword, Dad. I want to keep watching that arrogant prick out there to make sure he doesn't steal our car so you won't have a fucking excuse not to come get me and drive me home from where I'll be.

>>*NED starts off.*

KAREN
>Where are you going?

NED
>Just stay put. I'm going to go talk to him.

KAREN
>No don't do that ...

NED
> It's okay. I'll just find out what he's doing out there ... Then you won't have to be scared ... I'll be right back.
>
> *NED goes outside.*

KAREN
> Yeah you'll be right back unless he slits your fucking throat!
>
> (*watching*) Okay ... walking, walking, walking ... that's okay ... a little talking, that's fine ... just ... not so close ... You're too close! What's he—okay he's mad so just ... No don't push him! What is wrong with you!? Jesus!! Enough fucking pushing, okay!? You're gonna get ... Jesus!
>
> (*backs away and cups her hands*) Fight! Fight!! (*suddenly still*) Okay I wash my hands of the whole thing. (*sits in NED's chair, picks up the newspaper*) Just forget about it. It's got nothing to do with me.
>
> *GWEN rushes in, doing up her bathrobe.*

GWEN
> What's going on?

KAREN
> (*coldly*) Well where would you like me to start?
>
> *GWEN just looks at her.*
>
> *Blackout.*

Scene 2

Two comfortable chairs. GWEN sits across from VONNEGUT.

GWEN
It was the repo man. Guy came to repossess our car, Ned got all worked up and pretty much attacked him.

VONNEGUT
And the police came?

GWEN
Yeah. Apparently he might get charged with assault.

VONNEGUT
Apparently?

GWEN
Well I had other things on my mind. I mean I knew things were tight, but all of a sudden our vehicle was being taken away …

VONNEGUT
So it was a shock …

GWEN
Well the neighbours were out on their lawns by then, so it was also pretty embarrassing. Not that I care about what they all think.

VONNEGUT
Except we've already established that you do. You wouldn't let Ned tell them he lost his job …

GWEN
Not because I care about what they— Can you cut me a little slack here. Throwing things I might have said or done in my face doesn't really— And fuck them anyway. They'll probably all be in the same boat pretty soon.

VONNEGUT
Does it make you feel better to think that?

GWEN
Yeah. It does.

VONNEGUT
Well I think that's probably natural. Misery loves company, right.

GWEN
Except I'm not miserable, I'm mad.

VONNEGUT
I know. I was just—

GWEN
Ned's miserable.

VONNEGUT
Is he?

GWEN
You can't tell that from how I've described him and some of his … actions? He comes across all sunshine and happiness to you, does he?

VONNEGUT
> Well it sounds like he's coping.

GWEN
> It does? Maybe you should start paying closer attention. You know, actually listen to what I'm saying.

VONNEGUT
> I'm sorry. I sometimes get distracted.

GWEN
> By what?

VONNEGUT
> The state of the world usually.

GWEN
> Yeah but this is my time. So try to pay attention. When we're not together you can fret as much as you want about all that stuff.

VONNEGUT
> I'm sorry ...

GWEN
> Where were we.

VONNEGUT
> You're mad ...

GWEN
> Yes I am.

VONNEGUT
> At everything, everyone? At Ned, Karen ... Barnie?

GWEN
> Barnie's our dog. Why would I be mad at our dog? What are you, an idiot.

VONNEGUT
> Sorry ... not Barnie. I meant your son ... what's his—

GWEN
> Alex. His name's Alex. And I'm not mad at him. It's been so long since I've seen him I don't have any feelings about him at all.

VONNEGUT
> There's no way that can be true.

GWEN
> You don't think? Well how about this then? I'm not mad at *anyone*. Mad is what I get before I get ... busy. I get mad at the dirt in the house and then I eradicate it. Right now I'm mad at how bad things are going for us and soon I intend to fix it.

VONNEGUT
> How?

GWEN
> I'm working on that.

VONNEGUT
> Working on a plan?

GWEN
> A plan, an approach, whatever ...

VONNEGUT
> A plan to get your husband's job back, to cure your schizophrenic daughter ... to reconnect to your long lost son.

GWEN
> Well someone has to do it. What's your suggestion. I just give up?

VONNEGUT
>No. I don't believe in giving up, you know that. But I don't think you should take it on all by yourself because—

GWEN
>How about you just give me some practical advice here?
>
>(*off his look*) You know, some kind of hint on how to make any of it a little better. I know that's not your preferred way of operating but just this once ... can you offer up something I can actually ... use?
>
>>*VONNEGUT thinks awhile then shrugs.*

GWEN
>Well no harm asking ... (*stands*) Are you going to be writing about me? My story?

VONNEGUT
>I doubt it. I'm working on a collection of short stories. And of course, I'm dead so I'm not sure how that will affect my output.

GWEN
>You had to throw that in, eh. That part about you being dead. Like I didn't know that. Like I'm deluded or something and I don't really understand the nature of this relationship here. You know what, sometimes I wonder why I even bother.
>
>>*She leaves.*
>>
>>*Blackout.*

Scene 3

NED is standing near a bathroom door. GWEN approaches.

GWEN
How long has she been in there now?

NED
An hour?

GWEN
Doing what?

NED
Well she started the shower ... then she turned it off. Then she turned it on again. On, off ... on, off ... five, six times. And then silence.

GWEN
Complete silence?

NED
Yeah.

GWEN
And what about you? Were you silent too? You didn't feel you should be trying to make contact?

NED
She doesn't like that.

GWEN
    I know but—

NED
    I'll do it if I have to, but I think we should wait a little longer.

GWEN
    An hour, Ned. That's a long time. She's got her medication in there, I don't know what else. We can't just—

NED
    I don't think she's going to all of a sudden start hurting herself.

GWEN
    Why not? Look at all the other things she's done in the last two years "all of a sudden."

NED
    I still think we should wait.

GWEN
    Yeah well ... that's you, isn't it.

KAREN
    (*from inside bathroom*) You should listen to him. I don't like people talking to me when I'm in the bathroom.

GWEN
    I know that. But you've been in there a long time, Honey.

KAREN
    I'll be out soon enough. An hour or two at the most. Try to be patient okay.

GWEN
   Okay sure … but what are you doing in there?

KAREN
   Well right now I'm talking to you.

GWEN
   Your dad heard the shower start running a few times. Is there a problem?

KAREN
   What kind of problem?

GWEN
   With the shower …

KAREN
   Well if he heard it running what could the problem be?

GWEN
   Well it stopped … so we were just wondering—

KAREN
   Is there a point to this conversation? Because I've told you a hundred times I don't like talking to you unless there's a specific issue to be discussed.

GWEN
   Well the … issue is that you're due to make an appearance in court this afternoon and—

NED
   (*taking her away a bit*) No. Don't.

GWEN
   Don't what?

NED
   Don't … harasss her.

GWEN
I'm sorry ... harass her?

NED
Okay I didn't mean ...

(*whisper*) Look just leave her alone. She sounds fine. And you heard her, she'll be out in an hour or two.

GWEN
So we should just wait ...

KAREN
Sounds like a good idea to me.

GWEN
Suppose she wants an hour or two more after that. Then maybe a few days or a couple of weeks ...

NED
Come on, Gwen ...

GWEN
No I'm just wondering ... at what point would you be willing to intervene?

NED
Look don't make this harder than it already is, okay.

GWEN
Sure ... as long as you stop trying to make it *easier* than it is. We have to get her into that courtroom this afternoon. If we don't take her there, they'll come and get her.

NED
No way ...

GWEN
They told me.

29

NED
> You mean arrest her?

GWEN
> Yes.

NED
> No. She won't be able to— I can't handle that.

GWEN
> I'm sorry? You can't handle it?

NED
> No I don't think so.

GWEN
> Jesus ...

NED
> What?

GWEN
> Jesus!

NED
> I have to be able to tell you when I can't handle things, Gwen.

GWEN
> Really?

NED
> Yeah ... especially the things I *really* can't handle like seeing my daughter dragged off to—

GWEN
> Why not Vonnegut?

NED
> What? Who?

GWEN
Vonnegut. Why not tell him what you really can't handle, and just spare me, okay. He seems to think you're doing fine.

NED
I'm sorry. I don't know who you're—

GWEN
The point is, you don't want anyone to think you're as messed up as you actually are.

NED
And how messed up is that, Gwen?

GWEN
I just think you better find your own Vonnegut and you'd better do it pretty damn soon.

NED
Is Vonnegut a doctor, Gwen. Are you seeing a ... therapist?

GWEN
I don't need a therapist.

NED
Neither do I.

KAREN
I think you should both reconsider that position.

GWEN
(*to NED*) Okay ... sure keep thinking you don't need an outlet for all that anger you've got bottled up ... at least until you get enraged and beat the crap out of the next poor bastard who annoys you. Then maybe we can address the issue again. In the

meantime I need you to help me get our daughter out of the bathroom ... So ...

GWEN pushes NED towards the door.

NED
Karen? I think you should do what your mother—

KAREN
Okay, Dad. Good try. But you both have to leave now.

GWEN
We can't do that.

KAREN
Sure you can. Just turn around and walk away.

GWEN
We have to get ready to go to court ... Did you hear me? We have to—

KAREN
I told you, we'll talk in a couple of hours. Three max.

GWEN
If we don't go there voluntarily, they'll come here and—

NED
Gwen ...

GWEN
They'll come here and make you—

KAREN
Okay I need you to go. Just go away. Go!

GWEN
    Karen—

KAREN
    You fucking stupid woman! I need you to go away! Go go go go go!

    GWEN throws up her arms and walks away.

NED
    (*to KAREN*) Sorry.

    NED follows.

KAREN
    (*listens*) Okay thanks ... I appreciate that. Honest.

    Blackout.

Scene 4

KAREN is in the prisoner's dock.

KAREN
Well first of all I don't think I really have this disease you keep referring to. I have something else. I don't have a name for it yet, but it's different from the one you're talking about. So I think we should stop using the one which refers to something I don't have until we know a little more about what I actually *do* have. That's the first thing. The second thing is I keep meeting up with people who have things wrong with them way worse than what I've got, but they never wind up in here with me. I'd like that to change. I'd like you to arrest them, put them in a cell, take them out of a cell to meet a doctor, put them back in a cell, take them out to meet another doctor and a lawyer and then put them back in a cell again until the judge has time to see them ...

(*a little curtsy*) Thank you, your Honour ... then put them back in a cell until it's time to go to the hospital and get needles. I want these people to be treated exactly the same way I'm treated or I can't hold on to any respect for your justice system. I have a list of these people. Up here.

(*points to her head*) This is it. The social worker I was supposed to have assaulted for no reason, but who asked me the same question at least eight times even though I told her that doing so was a form of aggressive threatening behaviour. The other social worker who got involved supposedly to help the first social worker, but who took the opportunity to hold me against a wall without my permission and ask me more questions as well as just *saying* things in an aggressive threatening manner ... The receptionist who called the police and wrongly described my behaviour to them on the phone, the police themselves—more questions I didn't like ... The people in the waiting room who looked at me with aggressive pity ... the people on the sidewalk who did the same, obviously I don't have their names, I'm just making a point by adding them.

(*thinks*) My mom and dad of course, for letting this happen to me ...

Several of my father's business associates who always talked too loud when they came over and leered at my breasts, two teachers who leered at my breasts, the driving instructor who leered at my breasts, the guy who sold me my computer who leered at my breasts, the guy who bought my computer who leered at my breasts, and— This is a longer list than I first thought. I need to rest awhile ...

Hangs her head.

Blackout.

Scene 5

NED, GWEN and VONNEGUT in the three comfortable chairs.

GWEN
(*points to NED*) What's he doing here?

VONNEGUT
You brought him.

NED
She thinks I need help coping.

VONNEGUT
I thought you were coping fine.

GWEN
Right, yeah. I remember now. I wanted to straighten you out about that. Ask him why he couldn't even stay in the courtroom with Karen yesterday. Stay with his daughter while she—

NED
I was afraid …

GWEN
Who wasn't. It was not a nice experience. She looked very alone in that place …

VONNEGUT
How'd she do?

NED
> She had a few issues with how she was being treated …

GWEN
> She kinda went over the top.

NED
> (*to VONNEGUT*) Listen before we go any further I'd just like to say how much I admire your work.

KAREN
> He doesn't care. He's dead.

VONNEGUT
> Even so, it was a nice thing to say. Where's Karen now?

NED
> They put her in the hospital for another assessment.

GWEN
> I should have given her a tranquilizer.

VONNEGUT
> You do that sometimes?

GWEN
> Yeah I put it in her coffee or something.

VONNEGUT
> Do you think that's wise?

GWEN
> Is that a judgment?

VONNEGUT
> No. A question.

NED
> He just means it might not be good for her.

GWEN
> I don't do it for her. I do it for me.

VONNEGUT
> Nevertheless—

GWEN
> Is this going to be a lecture? Because as a lecturer you were a better writer.

VONNEGUT
> I always thought they were more or less the same thing ... just talking to people about the horrible mess we're leaving for future generations.

GWEN
> Yeah yeah sure but I really need to talk about the horrible mess *I'm* in right now.

NED
> I think that's a bit of an overstatement.

GWEN
> I'm starting to regret bringing you.
>
> (*to VONNEGUT*) I feel like it's a horrible mess. And I feel like I'm entitled to express that. My life ... my life with Karen can get pretty—

NED
> You mean when I'm at work?

GWEN
> You don't go to work anymore, remember.

NED
> I mean when I'm not here ...

GWEN
> Well since you lost your job you're always here ...
> (*looks at him suspiciously*) Unless you're not ...
>
> (*to VONNEGUT*) I think he just ... goes away a lot of the time. Just drifts off on us. I mean he's here, he can answer questions by rote, "did you buy bread, where's the paper?" ... but really ...

VONNEGUT
> (*to NED*) That true?

NED
> What?

GWEN
> What I just said ... You drift off.

NED
> Well ... I wouldn't call it drifting off. I've got a lot to think about.

VONNEGUT
> You mean things you'd *prefer* to think about?

NED
> I'm sorry?

VONNEGUT
> Besides your daughter and her—

NED
> I need to think about how I'm going to restart my career.

VONNEGUT
> Really. Is that even possible?

GWEN
> That's not a question he likes very much.

NED
> I still have contacts.

VONNEGUT
> But aren't most of them out of work too.

GWEN
> Doesn't like to hear that either.

NED
> Because it's not true. Not entirely. There are still a few—

GWEN
> It's just all too weird anyway. We're almost broke, and he thinks he can restart a career as a financial adviser.
>
> (*to NED*) What are you going to tell your clients? "Just don't do it the way I did it, and you'll be fine"?

VONNEGUT
> What do you want him to do?

GWEN
> Carpentry. He can start small, replace our kitchen cabinets.

NED
> She wants me to stay home with Karen.

GWEN
> (*to VONNEGUT*) It's time ...

NED
> She's pretty burned out. I understand that, but—

GWEN
> We don't need to go into all the whys and everything else. It's just time. I'm ready to go back to work.

NED
> Which is also something I understand—

GWEN
> He's very understanding. He just doesn't want it to happen.

NED
> I'm pretty sure we can't live on a teacher's salary.

GWEN
> Well right now we're living on just about nothing.

NED
> Which of course is just temporary.

GWEN
> Just like it's been for a year and a half ...

VONNEGUT
> Okay this is something—

GWEN
> We need to talk about? Sure ... But I've pretty much made up my mind this is how it has to be.

VONNEGUT
> Because of money?

GWEN
> Money. Sure.

VONNEGUT
> Not just Karen? Even if Ned got something say tomorrow, you'd still—

NED
> She'd still want out. (*to* GWEN) Wouldn't you?

GWEN
> And you will too, pal. There will come a time when even your bottomless well of love and concern for her will get sucked dry.

> *NED and GWEN just look at each other.*

VONNEGUT
> Is that what's happened to you, Gwen?

GWEN
> (*shrugs*) I don't know. Yes.

NED
> What?

GWEN
> Yes. That's what's happened to me. (*to* VONNEGUT) I'm afraid …

VONNEGUT
> Of?

GWEN
> All the things I don't know about her, which is really … everything. I mean she was twenty-three and normal and then she was twenty-four and … not. She was someone else. Who? And who was she when she was gone all that time, what did she do? Sometimes the things she says to me … the way she looks at me—

VONNEGUT
> Just you?

NED
> No, me too.

GWEN
> No no, not like that. The way she looks at me is ...
> (*to VONNEGUT*) Anyway I'm afraid of other things too. Losing the house, living on the street, starving to death ... so going back to work is the best thing, really ...
> (*to NED*) And as soon as possible ...

NED
> Well ... I guess that's it then.
> (*extending a hand to VONNEGUT*) It's been an unbelievable thrill to meet you. *Slaughterhouse Five* was one of the most memorable things I've ever read. Read twice, in fact. And *Cat's Cradle, Breakfast of Champions* ...
>
> > *GWEN grabs NED's hand.*

GWEN
> (*to VONNEGUT*) He won't be coming with me anymore.

NED
> Why not? Why not?
>
> > *GWEN is pushing him out.*
> > *Blackout.*

Scene 6

>   *GWEN on the living room couch brushing KAREN's hair.*
>   *KAREN is on the floor in front of her.*

GWEN
   This is nice … just sitting here like this together … calmly.

KAREN
   (*has been thinking*) Can I ask you a question … why do you think I became a prostitute?

GWEN
   What?

KAREN
   No I can't remember exactly what it was that made me decide to—

GWEN
   You're not a prostitute.

KAREN
   Not now. But I was.

GWEN
   When? When were you a prostitute?

KAREN
   Back when men were fucking me for money …

GWEN
> And when was that, Karen?

KAREN
> Back when I was a *prostitute*, Mom. You know, when I was on the street, outside your jurisdiction.

GWEN
> There was never any discussion of ... none of your social workers ever said anything about you being—

KAREN
> Well I didn't use my real name.

GWEN
> What name did you use?

KAREN
> Yours.

GWEN
> Karen—

KAREN
> I used your name. I thought it sounded more like a prostitute's name. Gwen ... I was a crack-whore who sucked cocks in parked cars ... and my name was ... Gwen.

GWEN
> Is this about hurting me? Because that's how it feels.

KAREN
> Why do want to make it about you? Why is everything about you?

GWEN
> Actually most things are about you, Honey.

KAREN

(*turns and slides away a bit*) Well if that was true, and remembering that I began this conversation with a question, why didn't you just fucking answer it, and not get into all that denial bullshit and how it "feels" like I'm hurting you.

GWEN

Can I smoke?

KAREN

If you stand at the door.

GWEN

Thanks …

GWEN takes out cigarette and heads off stage to the door.

KAREN

You know, I'm sick of telling you how much damage you're doing to yourself with those things.

GWEN

Does that mean you're going to stop telling me?

KAREN

Yes. Maybe it does …

GWEN

Okay … I've appreciated the concern though.

KAREN

I don't really understand anything you say, you know that? Not on any deep level. It's all just words … and attitude. Try to remember I'm doing this without medication. I've taken a very difficult road here, and it takes a toll.

GWEN
> It certainly does.

KAREN
> I meant on *me*!

GWEN
> Well to be honest, Honey—

KAREN
> Yes yes yes, I know it'd be easier for you if I used drugs. Much easier.

GWEN
> (*back on*) And is that why you won't?

KAREN
> Okay that's an example of something I can't really understand the entire meaning of. It sounds aggressive and a little mean. But maybe that's just the way it sounds.

GWEN
> I'm sorry. I just meant ... well why does it have to be so difficult ... for you. If the pills made it even a little easier to ... take a rest from everything. The voices ...

KAREN
> What voices?

GWEN
> ... and the fears ...

KAREN
> What fears?

GWEN

> (*moving closer*) You have to be back in court tomorrow.

KAREN

> Why was I a prostitute?

GWEN

> I want you to take something that will help it go a little easier …

KAREN

> Were you ever a prostitute? Is it something in my blood?

GWEN

> I was never a prostitute. I was a teacher, then a wife, then a mother. Those are the only things I've ever been. So if you really were a prostitute, I'm pretty sure it had nothing to do with me.

KAREN

> I'm not saying it's anything you did intentionally. I'm just not ready to totally absolve you of responsibility.

GWEN

> For anything?

KAREN

> (*thinking*) Money or love. It was either about money or love that made me do it.

GWEN

> Well before you ran away from home you had plenty of both.

KAREN
> Hmm. And you had parties, didn't you. Lots of parties, with lots of friends …

GWEN
> Yes we did …

KAREN
> Where are they now? The friends? I scared them all away?

GWEN
> Not the ones that mattered.

KAREN
> And where are they, the ones that mattered?

GWEN
> Busy. They're all very busy.

> *KAREN just looks at her.*

KAREN
> Just warning you, I'm going to have to cause a fuss if that judge wants to send me to jail for something I didn't do.

GWEN
> (*sitting closer to her*) Several people in that shelter saw you attack that woman and those social workers.

KAREN
> That woman was poisoning my food. Things were being put in my food and I had convincing evidence she was behind it.

GWEN
> You put her in the hospital.

KAREN
> I don't think so. Which hospital? Is she still there?

GWEN
> Yes she is. She's been there for several months now ...

KAREN
> Because of something I did? No no ... (*standing*) Let's go ...

GWEN
> Where?

KAREN
> To the hospital. I want to look at her charts. I bet it has nothing to do with me. She was an alcoholic, you know. It's probably the bitch's liver. Let's go.

GWEN
> We can't ...

KAREN
> Why not. I just want confirmation. Because if I get unjustly put in jail when all I was doing was confronting someone who was trying to kill me, I'm going to have to cause a huge motherfucking fuss.

GWEN
> Well first of all they can't put you in jail.

KAREN
> No? Well what was that place with all the bars on it then?

GWEN
> That's before you were assessed. They know now that you're too sick for jail. But if you get all worked up ... then they're going to want to medicate you.

KAREN
>   They can't—

GWEN
>   Yes they can. The law says if you present a danger to yourself or anyone else they can—

KAREN
>   Okay I'm outta here.
>   *She starts out.*

GWEN
>   (*grabbing her*) No you can't—

KAREN
>   Sorry. Gotta go.

GWEN
>   Karen if you don't show up—

KAREN
>   Not showing up is the best choice. If I don't show up nothing happens. I'll just get on with my life.

GWEN
>   How?

KAREN
>   Well I'm a prostitute so money won't be an issue. Now let go.

GWEN
>   No ...

KAREN
>   Let go!

GWEN
>   I can't.

KAREN
    (*angry*) Sure you can!

       She gives GWEN a mighty push, sending her flying.

KAREN
    See? I'm strong. I'll be fine!

       KAREN hurries out.

       Blackout.

Scene 7

> GWEN *and* NED *on the couch.* GWEN *cradled in* NED*'s arms. A drink in her hand.*

NED
She'd never intentionally hurt you. You know that.

GWEN
No. I don't. (*drinks*) And neither do you.

NED
(*flicks the glass*) Is that your first?

GWEN
She told me she was a prostitute.

NED
That's what made you want to drink? She's not a prostitute.

GWEN
Not now. Before. (*looks at him*) Was she? (*drinks*) Did you know?

(*sits up*) Did you? You did, didn't you? … for Chrissake, Ned … did you or didn't you?

NED
It came up a few times …

GWEN
What the hell does that mean? It "came up."

NED
> At that first hearing you weren't at …

GWEN
> You mean the one you didn't tell me about.

NED
> Yeah that one. It came up that she'd been picked up a few times—

GWEN
> For soliciting …

NED
> Yeah …

GWEN
> And why would you think I wouldn't want to know that?

NED
> Why would I think you *would*? I mean you never asked … Me, her social workers, anyone. So I figured you didn't want to know.

GWEN
> Maybe I just didn't want to ask … She also told me she was a crack addict.

NED
> For someone in her condition that's called self-medicating.

GWEN
> Really. You hear that at the hearing too?

NED
> No that's common knowledge.

GWEN
> Common knowledge …

NED
> For anyone who wants to know …

GWEN
> Know what?

NED
> Know what their runaway mentally ill daughter might be up to.

GWEN
> Okay that's not fair!

NED
> Yes it is. You didn't want to know! So until just now when it was thrown in your face you *didn't* fucking know!

GWEN
> You don't think so? You really think I didn't have any idea about all the bad rotten things that might be happening to her out there.

NED
> So why not talk about it?

GWEN
> I did.

NED
> Not with me.

GWEN
> No … with … someone else.

NED
> Who?

GWEN
> What's it matter?

NED
> Who?!

GWEN
> ... Vonnegut.

NED
> Who.

GWEN
> You know ... Kurt ... Vonnegut.

NED
> The writer? The *dead* writer?

GWEN
> Yeah well, you know how much I liked him, how much of him I used to read ...

NED
> Yeah me too, but—

GWEN
> Yeah it was one of our shared interests ... one of the things we—

NED
> You *talk* to him?!

GWEN
> Yeah ... so do you.

NED
> What?

GWEN
    Well just once ... I took you last time, but it didn't work out. You were kind of sycophantic.

NED
    Oh ...

    (*remembering*) So that's what you meant ... when you said I should get my own ... You were telling me to get my own imaginary Vonnegut.

GWEN
    Yeah or ... you know ... someone.

    She takes a drink. He just looks at her. He stands and starts out, stopping to look at her again before he leaves.

    Blackout.

Scene 8

VONNEGUT on a park bench. NED comes on wearing a pastry chef's uniform. VONNEGUT is in a suit.

NED
  (*looking around*) If this isn't nice, I don't know what is. (*smiles at VONNEGUT*) Who said that?

VONNEGUT
  I did?

NED
  (*nodding*) A Man Without a Country ... I think there's more to it though.

VONNEGUT
  Probably. I wasn't exactly pithy.

NED
  Who needs pith when you have poetry. Who said that?

VONNEGUT
  You did. Just now.

NED
  It's being with you, I think. Makes me want to say things that are quotable.

VONNEGUT
  Then I think you should try a little harder.

NED
> Yeah. Try a little harder. That's probably something I need to keep in mind ... just about things in general.

VONNEGUT
> You don't think you try hard enough about things in general.

NED
> No I'm just saying you can always try a little harder.

VONNEGUT
> Or maybe you can't.

NED
> Yeah that's true too. Sometimes you just have to say the hell with it, I've done my best. Wow. This is great. This exchange we're having of ...

VONNEGUT
> Contradictory thoughts?

NED
> Yeah whatever. It's gonna really help me work things out. I mean I know it's not what Gwen wanted ...

VONNEGUT
> She probably wanted you to find someone of your own.

NED
> Yeah and I thought about that. I went through a few of the more obvious choices.

VONNEGUT
> God?

NED
> Yeah but that's never been a very satisfying relationship. I usually just started begging

VONNEGUT
> Most people call it praying.

NED
> It felt like begging ... Anyway then I thought about my mother.

VONNEGUT
> You were right to leave her out of it. She's done enough for you.

NED
> I know ... So I moved on to a few other writers I'd enjoyed ... that had made me laugh, cry.

VONNEGUT
> Mostly laugh though, right?

NED
> Something wrong with that?

VONNEGUT
> Not unless you need a good cry as well.

NED
> Which I think I might.

VONNEGUT
> And that's what brought you back to me.

NED
> Exactly. Laughter and tears ... the "emotional cocktail of life ..." (*looks at VONNEGUT expectantly*) Better?

VONNEGUT
   A little.

NED
   And anyway, who is Gwen to claim ownership of you. I'm the one who found you first. She's always done that, by the way ... claimed things that actually belonged to me.

VONNEGUT
   What things?

NED
   Not ... things really. Feelings, thoughts, points of view even. I always figured it was her way of getting close to me. Now I think she just wants to absorb whatever's valuable about me ... so that I can just disappear without being missed.

VONNEGUT
   Wow.

NED
   Yeah ...

   (*a thought*) You mean "wow" that she's doing something like that, or wow that I think she is?

VONNEGUT
   "When you find yourself feeling even a little happy, don't be afraid to look around and say, if this isn't nice I don't know what the hell is." That's the whole quote, I think.

NED
   Yeah ... I guess I should be getting back.

VONNEGUT
   You should have eaten something.

NED
> I was just thinking that.

VONNEGUT
> I know ...
>
> (*smiles*) That uniform has a long and glorious tradition, by the way ... I mean just in case you're feeling silly about wearing it.

NED
> Just a little ...

VONNEGUT
> Part function, the reversible double-breast to hide stains, part image ... the white denoting kitchen cleanliness ...

NED
> And the checkered pants?

VONNEGUT
> Just for fun? ... Are you having fun, by the way?

NED
> Good question. Thanks. Maybe. I mean pastry chef wasn't my first choice, but the general culinary arts course seemed too ... intense. And I've come to like making cakes quite a lot.

VONNEGUT
> Enough to make a career of it?

NED
> Another good question. Boy, you're really tuned in ... A career? Well I have to do something, don't I. I mean losing the house was bad enough but now even coming up with rent on that pissy little apartment is getting tough ... And Gwen hasn't

been able to find anything. Apparently there's a glut of Latin teachers out there. Go figure. (*stands*) I really have to get going. We're doing creme caramel this afternoon, and I hear it's a bitch.

VONNEGUT
We haven't talked about Karen.

NED
Karen's lost. The police have given up on finding her. She's lost for good this time, I think.

VONNEGUT
That's what you're afraid of, not what you believe.

NED
Fears are much more powerful than beliefs.

VONNEGUT
(*nods*) That one's worth remembering.

NED
You mean you think it's true.

VONNEGUT
I don't know what's true ... just what's worth remembering.

NED
I like that too.

NED starts off. Stops. Looks back to VONNEGUT.

NED
My daughter's lost. That's what I'm afraid of *and* what I believe. I fear and believe my wife is somewhere between where she was and where she'll wind up. I only have fears and beliefs in those fears.

I *know* nothing … except that I know nothing. Nothing that can help either of them …

(*starting off*) Nothing to make it look like I'm even trying.

He is gone.

Blackout.

Scene 9

KAREN in a park, looking pretty rough. And she is high on crack, talking to people we can't see.

KAREN

(*to herself, quietly*) What's she ... what's she ... looking at ... what's the fuck ...

(*more aggressive*) What the fuck you looking at? Filthy little cunt! Yeah you, bitch!! That's right!

(*to someone else*) Greasy skank better stop looking at me like that or I'll go over there and make her bleed. Yeah, hammer her 'til she bleeds.

(*to Skank*) That's right, bitch. Get your bony legs moving on outta my sight or you are gonna start to fucking bleed ... You hear me, you worthless little cunt!?

(*smiles, to someone else*) She heard me ... she's moving. She heard me really clear ...

(*to Skank*) Hey! Don't fucking stop! Who told you that you could stop. Just keep moving!

(*to Others*) She heard me.

(*moving around*) This is my place! My place!! ... This is where I make my stand, and wait ... wait till it all gets to be what it's meant to be. Any of you want me for any purpose, this is where I am gonna be. You wanna sell me shit, I'm here. You wanna talk some shit, I'm here. You wanna fuck me I'm here ... I'm here to be used, loved, and even fucking ignored if that's the way it's meant to be. I just gotta know ... That's all. I just gotta know ...

(*she sits on a bench, looks around*) Okay, Shhh ... I think something's gonna happen now ... I think I can hear it about to happen.

(*gets a little smaller*) It's dark and I'm afraid ... I just remembered to be afraid ... I just remembered how bad it is out here. I don't want to be here alone. I just remembered I really don't want to be here.

Blackout.

Scene 10

NED in a light, alone.

NED
I didn't make her sick. I never told her that her sickness was too much to deal with. I never thought it would be better without her and her sickness around us. Okay I did think that. But I never let her know I was thinking it. Except I think she did. Actually, I'm absolutely sure she did.

Pull out to reveal NED watching GWEN stand over KAREN's covered corpse on a gurney.

NED
I want to say something to her. (*moving in closer*) Is that okay? ... If I just talk to her—

GWEN
She's not here.

NED
Okay but I have to—

GWEN
If you want to say something to her, say it silently. I don't want to hear you talking to that beaten-up bloodied corpse like you think it's our daughter. She's gone.

NED
>But I need to let something out of me or I might—

GWEN
>I can't hear it! I can't hear you say anything, all right. No one can say anything about this to me ever!
>
>(*leaving*) Do you understand!? Ever!

>>*NED watches her then slowly takes the sheet away down from KAREN's face.*

NED
>(*inhales sharply*) ... Oh God ... who did this to you.
>
>(*tries to control himself*) ... I'm ... I need to talk to you. Just to say ... I'm sorry. I'm so ... sorry this happened to you ... all of it. I would have done anything to stop what you've had to go through. I would have died to stop it from happening to you ... even the smallest least harmful part and I know ... I know there were many many horrible terrifying parts for you ... I'm ashamed I couldn't do anything to help you ... and I'm worried you stopped knowing how much I cared for you and ... was proud of you ... for everything you did before this came on you but mostly after ... how you fought and tried to ... make some sense of it ... when there was no sense to be made ... it was just some awful goddamn thing that happened the way all the other goddamn awful things happen ... And ... I'm sorry but I *am* glad it's over. For you, not me. If it was always going to be like that for you ... then ... at least that's ... over.

>>*He just ... lets go.*
>>
>>*Blackout.*

Scene 11

> *GWEN and VONNEGUT are at the wake. They are both dressed in black. There are two photos of a younger healthier Karen around. GWEN is holding a drink. VONNEGUT is holding a drink and moving around looking at the photos of Karen.*

GWEN
    I never understood.

VONNEGUT
    Understood what?

GWEN
    She didn't like the way her meds made her feel ... like "someone she didn't know." But without them she was someone no one knew ... including her. I mean I never knew what was going on in her head. Never ...

VONNEGUT
    Do you want me to tell you?

GWEN
    Obviously.

VONNEGUT
    This is, of course, just ... speculation. But since that's all fiction really is—

GWEN
> It makes you an expert.

VONNEGUT
> I tried to kill myself once. So I also have that as a reference point. My state of mind at that time ... but what was going on in Karen's ravaged brain? A lot obviously. Fractured pictures and sounds and fragments and sometimes wholly formed ideas and arguments that passed like sandstorms through her head and then sometimes returned and played out in reverse. Things that were understood from her past were involuntarily replayed in revision while almost simultaneously the world around her screamed for her very critical attention. And she felt things, did she ever.
>
> Everything was important, potentially dangerous for sure, but also intensely ironic and inevitable ... everything and everyone ... you and Ned, for example.

GWEN
> When she knew who we were.

VONNEGUT
> You were whoever she thought you were at the time ...

GWEN
> I just wanted to be her mother.

VONNEGUT
> Whatever that means ... even to people who aren't schizophrenics.

GWEN
> "Hi, Honey ... how you feeling today?" "Anything interesting happen at school?" "Don't worry about what you're going to do with your life, just try to enjoy each day, be with your friends, try to make the best out of whatever comes your way."
>
> (*shrugs*) That's what it means. Being her mother ...
>> *NED has wandered over. He is a little drunk.*

NED
> Who are you talking to?
>> *VONNEGUT wanders away.*

GWEN
> Guess ...

NED
> He's here?

GWEN
> Well he was until you staggered over. I think you annoy him.

NED
> Bullshit. He thinks I'm great.

GWEN
> You been talking to him too?

NED
> Yeah. And he says I'm the real deal.

GWEN
> That doesn't sound like the Vonnegut I know.

NED
> That's because it's the Vonnegut *I* know.

GWEN
> More like some guy you'd meet in a bar. "You sound like the real deal to me, pal. Kind of guy a man wants to take a piss with in an alley A good long piss."

NED
> (*looks at her*) Jesus ...

GWEN
> What the hell does that mean anyway, "the real deal"?

NED
> A simple honest man with a pretty good brain who always tried his best even under the worst of circumstances ...

GWEN
> Sounds like something you want on your headstone.

NED
> You think you can remember it?

GWEN
> Probably not. Doesn't matter though, you're not going to have a headstone. You're gonna get burned up just like our daughter.

NED
> Hey!

GWEN
> What?

NED
> Don't *ever* say that again, okay! You talk about burning her up ever again and I'll punch you in your goddamn throat!

(*getting closer*) Okay?

GWEN
(*smiles*) Yeah, Tough Guy. You made your point.

NED
Good ...

GWEN
You're okay with the word cremate though, right? You just don't like the word *burn*. The image of her bursting into flames is just too—

NED
What the fuck is your problem?

GWEN
(*looks around*) Oh ... look at all the people who showed up. So many of your former colleagues ... Well they have a lot of time on their hands ...

NED moves away.

GWEN
What are you doing?

NED
I can't listen to you talk about her that way.

GWEN
(*approaching him*) I'm not talking about Karen. Just the way her body was ... disposed of.

NED
And that makes you feel better for some reason?

GWEN
No it makes me feel much worse. Not as bad as I'd like to feel, but at least it's a start.

(*looking again*) How about that. Some your little friends from the kitchen came along as well.

NED
"Little friends from the kitchen" … They're not elves. They're sous chefs.

GWEN
They cut up onions.

NED
Well in a few months they'll be cooking those onions in very inventive ways, and then they won't be giving you the time of day.

GWEN
Go away.

NED
Why?

GWEN
Because I want my writer friend back. He'll let me say whatever the hell I need to say on the day of my daughter's funeral. He'll let me use the words *burn* and *body* and *flesh* and any other goddamn thing I want or need to say to make me feel whatever it is I need to feel.

NED
You know, I might be your writer friend one day soon. (*leaving*) I think I've got a book in me.

GWEN
(*to herself*) It's about his pain and disappointment.

Her VONNEGUT returns, with a larger drink.

GWEN
> He's going to write a book about her ... and it'll just be all be about his pain and disappointment.

VONNEGUT
> I'll give you a hand if you want to beat him to it.

GWEN
> Mine wouldn't exploit my daughter's misfortune.

VONNEGUT
> Yes you have enough of your own misfortune to exploit, don't you.

GWEN
> I also have my own disappointment.

VONNEGUT
> I've been thinking a lot about disappointment lately.

GWEN
> So have I ...

VONNEGUT
> Which is more or less what I just said ... Anyway here are my thoughts on the subject. Screw it. We still have to live. As ... long as, you know ... we're alive.

GWEN
> Jesus ... you've been drinking ...

VONNEGUT
> Haven't we all ... (*looks around*) Any of these people friends of yours?

GWEN
> I don't have any friends. They didn't know how to deal with Karen ... or me.
>
> They didn't know how to deal with my feelings about Karen, they didn't know how to deal with my feelings, they didn't know how to deal with Ned losing his job—

VONNEGUT
> They didn't know how to deal with very much, did they.

GWEN
> I can't really blame them.

VONNEGUT
> That's a lie. I bet you're looking around right now wanting to set them all on fire.

GWEN
> You said it.

VONNEGUT
> You thought it.

GWEN
> I only thought it so you could say it ... you know, so I could hear what it sounds like.

VONNEGUT
> And?

GWEN
> It's better coming from you.
>
> *They both drink.*
>
> *Blackout.*

Scene 12

NED on the park bench. VONNEGUT comes on out of breath, putting on a sweater.

NED
You're late.

VONNEGUT
I wasn't sure if you wanted me to come.

NED
I thought I might need to be alone … then—

VONNEGUT
You changed your mind. I know. Next time I'll need a little more notice.

He sits next to NED.

VONNEGUT
What's wrong?

NED takes a gun out of his pocket.

NED
I bought this today. It's untraceable.

VONNEGUT
And the problem?

NED
Well the problem is what I want to do with it.

VONNEGUT
> Maybe just having it is the problem. If you got rid of it, then whatever you wanted to do with it would be irrelevant.

NED
> I don't think Gwen will ever be at peace until someone is made responsible for what happened to our daughter.

VONNEGUT
> It's not the kind of crime police usually solve. A homeless runaway prostitute—

NED
> I don't like her called that.

VONNEGUT
> I know. But from their point of view that's what she was.

NED
> Their point of view means nothing to anyone except them. They know very little about her life or who she was.

VONNEGUT
> And that's why they'll never work that hard to find out who killed her.

NED
> There are certain people, certain types she associated with—

VONNEGUT
> And you think one of them might have killed her?

NED
> Yeah well maybe they could be held responsible somehow. Some of them, any of them, all of them ... They're just people leading sad useless lives no one really cares about—

VONNEGUT
> Unless they have family too.

NED
> So maybe their families are also responsible ... for what they let their children become.

VONNEGUT
> Are you responsible for what Karen became?

NED
> Must be ... in some way. I'm definitely responsible for not doing enough to help her. Maybe I should just use this on myself. You think that would be enough for Gwen?

VONNEGUT
> Why don't you ask her?

NED
> (*shrugs*) She wouldn't be able to admit it.

VONNEGUT
> Yeah well ... if you decide to kill yourself, the most important thing is not to botch it. Take my word for it. No matter what else you accomplish in life, you'll always think of yourself as a failure.

NED
> I don't see how I could botch it. What's so hard about putting a gun in your mouth and pulling the trigger?

VONNEGUT
> Well you'll have to find that out for yourself. But exploring the issue from a moral standpoint, which is how I made my reputation, it would be better to do yourself in than go on a killing rampage of the under-class, which is what you first had in mind.

NED
> Although one of them probably did kill her.

VONNEGUT
> *One* of them.

NED
> *Any*one of them ... (*stands*) This is something I need to think more about.

VONNEGUT
> I know you're still upset about failing that chef's course.

NED
> It was all about the crème caramel. Everything else I could do just fine. My lemon tarts, also very difficult by the way, were actually a hit.

VONNEGUT
> And yet you didn't get your certificate.

NED
> No ... You think that actually has something to do with—

VONNEGUT
> There's a hell of difference between killing someone, even yourself, over your daughter's tragic death and doing it because you couldn't get your crème caramel not to scald.

NED
   Yeah. I hear you. (*he looks at the gun*) I better make sure.
   Blackout.
   Intermission.

Scene 13

GWEN and KAREN on a high-rise balcony in two rattan chairs. GWEN is in a bathrobe, hair not brushed. KAREN is nicely, almost demurely, dressed. KAREN is drinking tea. GWEN is drinking scotch.

GWEN
　I was never one of those people who needed to "understand" things. Things were just like this or just like that. People behaved ... the way they behaved. And that's the way it was. It was all ... just ...

KAREN
　Just the way it was ...

GWEN
　Yes. But I need to understand this. I need to understand what happened to you.

KAREN
　I got sick ...

GWEN
　That's it?

KAREN
　Pretty much ... I got sick. I became mentally ill, Mom. Everything flowed from that.

GWEN
　Yeah but what were you thinking?

KAREN
> When?

GWEN
> All the time ... what were you thinking ... about me? Did you have feelings for me?

KAREN
> Nothing pleasant.

GWEN
> Ever?

KAREN
> Well I didn't want to harm you or anything. I just ... well, you were either too close or too far away ... never just the right distance ... And your voice ...

GWEN
> Too loud?

KAREN
> Or that tiny trembling voice of concern. It sounded fake, and I hated it.

GWEN
> Well ... I guess I was just too sick with worry about you to get that just right. You know not too loud, not too trembling ...

KAREN
> Yeah ... and like I said, I was sick. So try not to take it personally. You like this dress?

GWEN
> I bought it for you ...

KAREN
> I never wore it.

GWEN
    I know. I wish you had.

KAREN
    I know (*points*) That won't help. Drinking won't help.

GWEN
    I think we're going to have to disagree about that, Honey. (*smiles*) Remember how we hardly used to disagree about anything.

    Books, clothes, politics. We liked all the same things. It was like we were the same person.

KAREN
    And now we actually are.

    (*smiles*) That must make you happy on some level ... I'm not saying you don't wish I was still alive.

GWEN
    (*nods*) But this is better than nothing.

KAREN
    How's Dad?

GWEN
    He flunked out of cooking school.

KAREN
    No fucking way. Unbelievable. What's his fucking problem?

GWEN
    Who knows ... I'm a little worried that we're going to just ... dissolve pretty soon.

KAREN
Dissolve the marriage?

GWEN
Yeah ... and then just dissolve.

KAREN
Marriages often fall apart after the loss of a child. You know that ... so you're probably just anticipating the worst.

GWEN
I've already experienced the worst. The marriage ending would just be ... unfortunate. I mean especially for your father. He loves me a lot.

KAREN
And you love him ...

GWEN
Yes of course I do. What I meant was—what did I mean?

KAREN
You think he's weak.

GWEN
No. Not weak. Weaker. Weaker than me.

KAREN
He might not be. He might be okay no matter what.

GWEN
That's an interesting thought. Thank you. We'll do this again, okay. I think we'll have to keep doing this for awhile.

KAREN
    No problem ... You might want to lay off the booze a little in the meantime.

GWEN
    Thank you for your ...

KAREN
    Concern ... It's just concern, Mom.

GWEN
    Yeah ...

    They drink. KAREN winces.

GWEN
    Too hot?

KAREN
    No ... it's fine.

GWEN
    You sure?

KAREN
    Yeah ...

GWEN
    You're sure.

KAREN
    Yeah!

    Blackout.

Scene 14

NED on a street corner walking back and forth. Wearing a sandwich board that reads: BIG BLOWOUT.

NED

Everything priced to sell! No offer rejected! All inventory must go, everything forty, sixty, eighty percent off. Some things almost free! Big big blow out ... everything must be sold. Buy now. Pay later. Much later. Whenever the fuck you want. Zero interest. Nothing down ... Just buy! Buy something. Buy a house, a car, a TV, a toaster, a wallet. Stop worrying and buy. It's not a bad thing or a good thing. It's just something that has to happen!

He stops pacing. Looks around, smiles.

NED

Am I happy to see all of you, or is that a gun I've got in my pocket? That's a question you should all be asking yourselves. Here are a few more. Ask yourselves what I'm capable of. How far I've come to get here. What I've left behind, what I've lost ... how desperate I am, how completely indifferent to the consequences of my actions I've become. And how little it would take for me to do something to make myself feel a little bit better including blowing some of your stupid useless fucking heads off!!

He starts to pace again

NED

    Big blowout. Big fucking blowout. Biggest motherblowing blowout of all time. Everything must go. And I mean everything!! It's just gotta fucking go!!

    He stops pacing.

NED

    I really want you to buy something just to keep things rolling ... just to keep it all moving along ... like before when everything seemed fine ... even when it wasn't ... So come on, buy a little something so everything can seem fine again.

    Don't need anything? Buy something for someone you love. Buy something for someone you want to love *you*. Buy something for someone you barely know, for the less fortunate, for the truly fucked up ... Buy something just to help out ...

    He starts to pace.

NED

    Big BLOW OUT!! Liquidation sale! Everything must go! Everything must be liquidated!!

    Blackout.

Scene 15

GWEN, still in her bathrobe and drink in hand, is sitting on a small folding chair. So is KAREN. VONNEGUT is sitting on a small crate. KAREN is gesturing to VONNEGUT, confused.

GWEN
    I don't like to drink alone.

KAREN
    (*to VONNEGUT*) I think she means she doesn't like to drink *while* she's alone.

VONNEGUT
    Is that why we're here?

GWEN
    I knew you'd understand. (*to KAREN*) He's smart. *And* compassionate.

KAREN
    The two traits you admire most.

GWEN
    When his sister died of cancer, he adopted her three children.

VONNEGUT
    I'm sure you would have done the same ...

KAREN
    (*to GWEN*) *Would* you have?

GWEN
    Probably not.

KAREN
    (*to VONNEGUT*) She doesn't like children that much.

GWEN
    They're pretty time consuming.

VONNEGUT
    She doesn't mean you. She means your brother …

GWEN
    (*to KAREN*) He's right. You were never a problem.

KAREN
    Until I became the biggest problem you ever had.

GWEN
    Well that's not something you did by choice though. Or is it? Just checking …

KAREN
    No … it's not.

GWEN
    No of course not. Your brother on the other hand—

KAREN
    (*to VONNEGUT*) Okay before she gets started, I should tell you she still loves the asshole.

VONNEGUT
    Maybe. But love doesn't help you understand someone. And she—

GWEN
    I didn't get him. I just didn't get him. I mean I was trying. I was busting my balls—

KAREN
> (*to VONNEGUT*) She really does think she has balls, by the way.

GWEN
> ... trying to figure out what the selfish little prick was all about. And then ... he was gone.

KAREN
> Yeah. He just fucked off. And I needed him.

GWEN
> He should have stayed to help.

KAREN
> (*to VONNEGUT*) Helped with me. She needed all the help she could get with me.

GWEN
> He just pissed off. Coward couldn't take it.

KAREN
> He liked things ... to be a certain way. He liked to be in control. He probably couldn't stand being around all that ... confusion.

GWEN
> Who the hell could? Fuck him.

KAREN
> (*to VONNEGUT*) She doesn't mean that.

VONNEGUT
> I think you should listen to her more closely. (*to GWEN*) Say it again.

GWEN
> We needed him, and he didn't give a shit. So yeah, fuck him and anyone else who treats their parents like that ...

(*drinks*) ... treats anyone like that.

VONNEGUT

When's the last time you got dressed? You should ask yourself what's going on with that? It's probably not that you don't like any of your clothes.

GWEN

You think it's time to stop my slide?

KAREN

I do.

GWEN

Don't worry about me, Doll. Your father's in much worse shape than I am. Actually ... we were talking about that last time I saw him ... kind of speculating about which one of us was taking it all the hardest.

VONNEGUT

(*to KAREN*) Like it's a competition or something.

GWEN

Well if it is, I'm pretty sure he's winning. He's really messed up. It's kind of embarrassing actually. I mean the things that come out of his mouth ... who can listen to that shit?

VONNEGUT

What shit?

GWEN

You know ...

VONNEGUT

I mean what shit in particular ...

GWEN

Nothing in particular ... just the way it comes out. No order to it, no structure ...

KAREN
    (*to VONNEGUT*) She likes structure. She taught Latin.

VONNEGUT
    No one cares.

GWEN
    Is he talking about the economy? The world in general? His own turmoil? The plight of the homeless? Who the hell can tell?
    (*looks around*) And in the meantime, we're living in smaller and smaller places ...

VONNEGUT
    On much smaller furniture ...

GWEN
    (*acknowledging chair*) Yeah ... (*to KAREN*) It's like we're ...

KAREN
    Disappearing ...

GWEN
    Yeah.

KAREN
    Does that worry you?

GWEN
    I'm not sure I care ... (*looks at them both, smiles*) I'm so glad you two get along.

    Blackout.

Scene 16

GWEN and NED on the street. GWEN is still in her bathrobe but is now also wearing a toque. NED is wearing a sign around his neck which reads: HOMELESS. OUT OF WORK. AND FUCKED UP. His chef's hat is on the ground in front of them. They are begging for change. GWEN is trying to hide behind something.

GWEN
    (*quietly*) Ned ... (*no response*) Ned!

NED
    What?

GWEN
    What's happening to us? We seem to be just letting it all—

NED
    I feel engaged.

GWEN
    You feel what?

NED
    Engaged. Fully engaged in the current circumstances.

GWEN
> Ours?

NED
> Everyone's. I feel completely engaged and in sync with the whole stupid mess which is the world right now. Both internally and externally.

GWEN
> (*to herself*) Lunatic ...

NED
> What?

GWEN
> (*approaching him*) You're talking like a lunatic. It's starting to get me down.

NED
> You mean I'm annoying you.

GWEN
> That too. But mostly you're depressing me.

NED
> I think you're more annoyed than you are depressed. I think you're just generally annoyed. I think you think we didn't deserve any of this and that it's all just so ... unfair.

GWEN
> If you're going to start ranting, especially if it's about me and what you think I think, all I ask is that you try to remain coherent.

NED
> As if coherence is the most important thing about a rant. You should stop trying to control whatever it is you think ... you're ... losing control of.

GWEN
> Which would be just about everything, right.

NED
> (*to a passing stranger*) Money! The hat is out for money. Nothing else. Not pity, not disdain. I wasn't trying to scare you. I just wanted money because we have to eat, fuck-face.

GWEN
> It's not his fault.

NED
> I never said it was.

GWEN
> It was implied. I think if we're going to do this—

NED
> Do what?

GWEN
> What we're doing.

NED
> Which is what?

GWEN
> Hanging on. If we're going to try to hang on until things improve—

NED
> Improve? Please.

GWEN
> The point is, we can't get bitter. We can't become the kind of people who are bitter about life's disappointments.

NED
> Well no offence, but you've seemed pretty bitter to me, darling.

GWEN
> Privately. But that's not the face we should be presenting to the public.

NED
> Because?

GWEN
> It's not who we are. We're just poor people.

NED
> Who were once pretty well off. So I think it's fair to expect some prolonged period of adjustment. I think the public will understand

GWEN
> Okay but I want to hold on to some of the things I admired about myself.

NED
> You mean before you started going everywhere in your bathrobe?

GWEN
> Or you began treating yourself like a blackboard? ... Yeah. I never blamed anyone for my disappointments.

NED
> Except me.

GWEN
> Well you were actually responsible for some of them, so yeah. But mostly—

NED
   I never blamed you for anything.

GWEN
   Which is probably because you didn't feel as close to me as I did to you.

   NED looks at her then turns and puts his hand out to a passerby.

NED
   Hey! Money! Just give us money. Or don't. But make the decision. Don't just walk by like we're not here. It's depressing.

GWEN
   (*to passersby, suddenly angry too*) He doesn't mean us. He means you . You're the ones who are depressing. Walking by like that ... it's not even human!

NED
   That's telling them.

GWEN
   (*starting off*) Let's try a different shelter tonight.

NED
   (*picking up hat*) Whatever you say Light of My Life ...

GWEN
   That last one ... I was sure we'd never make it through the night. You still have that gun?

NED
   (*pats his pocket*) You bet. Right in here.

GWEN
   And you're willing to use it to protect our lives.

NED
>Damn right I am. I told you, I'm totally engaged and in sync with the way of the world ...

He follows her off.

Blackout.

Scene 17

GWEN is on a cot in a shelter. VONNEGUT is on the next cot.

GWEN
(*looking around*) Increasingly uncomfortable. It really feels like ... poverty.

VONNEGUT
Or old age ...

GWEN
Except last night Ned and I had sex for the first time in ... months. We made love here on my cot in this sleeping bag ... surrounded by all these ... other people. I wish I'd been able to shower first ... but other than that, it was nice. Ned cried ... other than that, it was pretty good ... Right afterwards, I thought ... "This would be a good time to die ... Yeah that would be nice. Let's just die now."

VONNEGUT
Well he still has that gun so it's easy to contemplate.

GWEN
Which is good. I mean to have that option. Especially for him, I think. I mean he's still conscious. He still knows who he is ... He *feels* who he is and what's happening to us.

VONNEGUT
    And you're not ...

GWEN
    Well ... it's just a little bit like a bad dream for me, you know?. So many things that are just ...

    (*sees something*) Like for example ... (*gestures*) ... what the hell is that woman trying to pull over there?

    (*to Woman across the room*) Hello!? Don't do that! That's right. I saw you take them now just put them back!

VONNEGUT
    Tell her she'll feel immediately better about herself if she does it.

GWEN
    Really?

VONNEGUT
    Try it.

GWEN
    (*to Woman*) You might not believe this, but if you put those shoes that do not belong to you back you'll feel a hell of a lot better about yourself. Your whole life might turn around.

VONNEGUT
    That's probably a bit much ...

GWEN
    (*to Woman*) At least you won't have to feel like such a shit when you see that elderly lady struggling around without her shoes ... Oh nice ...

(*to VONNEGUT*) You see that? How did that gesture become so popular. And not just with low-life thieves like that asshole ... Everyone flips the bird. "Flips the bird" ... Sounds almost as disgusting as it looks ... Childish, ugly ... stupid. It's all so ... nasty. You know what I think may be happening? I think Ned might be right. It could all be falling apart.

VONNEGUT
Because people are giving each other the finger?

GWEN
It's symptomatic ... how can it all hold together with people showing so little regard for each other ...

(*to Woman across the room*) Put the freakin' shoes back, and stop staring at me. Or I'll *give* you something to stare at!!

(*to VONNEGUT*) Whatever that means ...

VONNEGUT
But she got your point. Look ...

GWEN
Yeah ...

(*to Woman*) Okay ... now don't you feel better? Sure you do. Have a nice day. See you at dinner.

(*giving her the finger*) Same to you!

> GWEN *gives a few other people in the shelter the finger, two fingers. She and* VONNEGUT *giggle and give each other the finger repeatedly*
>
> *Blackout.*

Scene 18

Park bench. NED and KAREN. KAREN looks great in jogging gear, her hair pulled back. NED is leaning his chin on a picket sign which reads, "FIGHT THE POWER."

NED
　　Barnie died.

KAREN
　　When?

NED
　　Don't know exactly. He couldn't come with us when we moved into that apartment so we asked the Wheelers to take him. Do you remember them?

KAREN
　　He leered at my breasts. She asked me how I was feeling a lot. "How are you feeling today? Any better?"

NED
　　Called them up just to see how he was doing. "Not so good," said Sam. "He's dead." "Not so good ... he's dead." Like making a joke about my dog dying was an appropriate thing to do. First thing I thought was "Why Barnie, why not you, Sam?" Truth is I didn't just think it ... I actually *said* it. So

103

Sam hung up ... Then I thought, "Why Barnie, why not *me*?"

KAREN

It's not your time.

NED

You think there's a time?

KAREN

You don't? Maybe you'd feel comforted if you did.

NED

As long as I can choose it. You going for a run?

KAREN

(*looks at her clothing*) I guess.

NED

I wish you'd kept it up. Running. I always thought if you'd kept it up you could've run right past your problems. Just powered through ...

KAREN

That's kind of dumb, Dad.

NED

Yeah. But when you were running and playing sports you were so healthy ... Then you stopped.

KAREN

Because I got sick.

NED

Yeah. Or ... maybe you got sick after you stopped.

KAREN

Except I didn't. I stopped because I got sick.

NED
> Are you sure?

KAREN
> Yes.

NED
> Why aren't *I* sure?

KAREN
> Because you're not sure of anything anymore. You've lost your sense of ...

NED
> My sense of sureness ...

KAREN
> Yeah. I think maybe that's why you've become a sloganizer. "Fight the Power." What's that mean exactly?

NED
> I think it's pretty self-evident.

KAREN
> What power? Fight how?

NED turns the sign around. The other side says, "BE THE POWER."

KAREN
> Be the power?

NED
> Yes, indeed. Fight the power by becoming the power. You have to admit it's good advice. It's much better than the advice I used to give, "Diversify your portfolio." "Maximize your growth potential." What a bunch of shit ... Well are you going to run or not?

KAREN
> I will if you want me to.

NED
> Don't do it just for me.

KAREN
> Why not.

NED
> It has to be for you.

KAREN
> Since when. Just about everything I ever did I did because you or Mom wanted me to.

NED
> Is that true?

KAREN
> Why would I lie?

NED
> So you were always trying to please us.

KAREN
> Except for the times I hated both your guts and didn't give a shit what you thought.

NED
> You mean when you got sick.

KAREN
> No when I turned thirteen.

NED
> Yeah those were a rough couple of years …

KAREN
> Well not compared to the nightmare that was heading our way. (*points to her head*) The voices ... they fucked it all up for us, didn't they?

NED
> I'm just wondering—

KAREN
> Dozens of them all telling me some crazy shit, making me do some crazy shit ... loud screeching crazy people in my head just not stopping, never stopping unless I got so cranked up I couldn't think straight. Man ...
>
> (*looks at him*) You're wondering what?

NED
> If feeling you always had to please us maybe is one of the reasons you—

KAREN
> People usually feel that they have to please someone. Why not you. Or Mom.
>
> If I hadn't become a basket case I probably would have gotten married to some guy I had to please, had kids I had to please, friends, co-workers ...

NED
> Or maybe you could've just run through all that.

KAREN
> That's a nice thought, Dad.

NED
> Yeah, well ... if I can't keep having nice thoughts about you, Honey ... you know, seeing you in these clothes, looking so healthy ... well I might have to

just ... end it. Because what would be the purpose of going on, you know?

KAREN

(*points to sign*) Well there's that sign ... I'm sure there are a lot of people you haven't reached yet.

NED

And I've got others. They're at the shelter. I take a new one out everyday. I mean I rotate. There are nine of them. You know, to cover all the days of the week.

KAREN

There are seven days in a week.

NED

Plus the two other ones.

KAREN

Two extra signs?

NED

Two extra days. The ones nobody is doing anything with. (*off her look*) Well ... you can't really blame them. They're in another dimension.

> *NED gives KAREN a look then gestures for her to run. She smiles, jogs off.*
>
> *Blackout.*

Scene 19

GWEN is on her cot in the shelter surrounded by shoes. VONNEGUT is on the next cot eating a banana.

GWEN
I've never seen you eat before.

VONNEGUT
In all the photos, they wanted me to either smoke or just sit there looking sad and troubled. It always looked so fake to me. I'd tell them "Let me suck on a milkshake or something. Anything normal."

GWEN
Fakery sells. Fakery sells better than anything really.

VONNEGUT
That's only because honesty isn't marketed very well. (*gestures to shoes*) Good idea you had there.

GWEN
We were supposed to take turns guarding the shoes while everyone else slept. This is my third night in a row. I don't really object ... It gives me something to do.

VONNEGUT
Guarding shoes is enough to occupy your mind?

GWEN

    Well I can't sleep anyway. Ned is out till all hours dispensing his "advice."

VONNEGUT

    Not many people out there at this hour to receive it though …

GWEN

    He says the ones who need it the most are. I think he's up to something.

VONNEGUT

    Prowling for sex?

GWEN

    No he gets enough of that from me now. We just get into a sleeping bag and screw our brains out. Any time at all, no matter who's around … who's watching, who's listening. We don't care.

VONNEGUT

    Swell!

GWEN

    Except I'm not sure why. You have any thoughts?

VONNEGUT

    Well you've lost so many other things … why not a few inhibitions?

GWEN

    I suppose we'll be doing it in the park or at a bus stop next … I mean if we ever need to take a bus to someplace. Can't imagine where that would be … He's up to something, I can feel it. This isn't the worst it can get, you know. It can get a lot worse.

VONNEGUT
    Oh I know that. Things could all get so bad you won't even recognize where you are. It won't seem like the same planet.

GWEN
    Really?

VONNEGUT
    You won't recognize anyone around you. They won't seem like human beings. They won't behave like human beings or even house pets.

GWEN
    Jesus ...

VONNEGUT
    ... and they'll all be ... hungry. Hungry ... undomesticated in any way ...

GWEN
    Okay that's—

VONNEGUT
    That means they'll eat anything ... even each other.

GWEN
    Please ...

VONNEGUT
    That will be the norm, actually. Cannibalism is probably going to be the norm in the era of the worst of things.

GWEN
    Please stop ...

VONNEGUT
> Sure. I just wanted you to know it could be a lot worse than the worst you think it could be.

GWEN
> So I could appreciate what I have?

VONNEGUT
> Which isn't much, granted.

GWEN
> But at least I'm not being eaten.

VONNEGUT
> Exactly. Now talk some more about sex.

> *Blackout.*

Scene 20

NED under a light on a street corner, wearing a sign which reads: "WHO IS RESPONSIBLE?" He appears to be addressing a small crowd.

NED

I thought I could stop wanting to know there for awhile. But I can't. I need to know. Don't tell my wife. She's the one in the bathrobe. But I need to know, and I need your help. It's probably someone like you. Fucked up like you. Unsure, alone, confused, desperate, sad, angry ... hungry ... hungry for love, for a little affection, for the tiniest bit of concern ... and relief ... hungry for relief ...

(*moves closer to the crowd*) ... from knowing what *you* did ... which was stab a very sick young woman twenty-six times. Five in the heart, twelve in the torso ... and the rest on the face ... So just let me know who you are, okay.

(*takes out his gun*) And I'll do my part by putting you out of your misery ... help you out of this mistaken life, this failure of a life which I'm sure is not all your fault but still ... has to end. End before you cause any more pain ... pain so bad it sucked the air out of my lungs, ripped away at my heart, and left me gasping and wanting to die. So if you're out there, and you want relief, you know where to find me. And if there's anyone else who thinks that they should just be … removed from the picture, I'm willing to help. I'm especially interested in people like my former bosses, people who in pursuing their own unbelievably selfish interests have basically ruined the world. I can't get to you, for obvious reasons. I can't penetrate your enclaves or sneak into your boardrooms, but, if by any miracle you develop a conscience and go in search of your just punishment, I'm here. And in the meantime, getting back to you violent fuckups, maybe I should put a few of you out of your misery right away to save us from whatever hell you've got in store for the rest of us … Just please don't tell my wife any of this, except for that one part about helping. She'll put a positive spin of her own on that. She's become strangely upbeat lately … although that's not even slightly reflected in how she dresses.

He puts the gun away. For now.

Blackout.

Scene 21

GWEN and KAREN in the shelter. Staring at each other from different cots. KAREN is in her dress. GWEN is in Karen's track suit.

KAREN
    You're wearing my track suit.

GWEN
    Is that okay?

KAREN
    There was a time it would have made me think someone was trying to steal my life ... take my clothes and then take my life ... use it themselves, give it to someone else ... It was just a useless thing anyway, my life ... what did it matter what was done with it? That's what I would have thought.

GWEN
    I know ...

KAREN
    No. Don't cry ... It's okay now.

GWEN
    No ... it's not.

KAREN
    I mean you wearing my track suit. I like it now. I mean it's okay now.

(*looking around*) You know, you should probably get out of this place. Any plans to do that?

GWEN
   Not at the moment.

KAREN
   But maybe you should be somewhere better … Maybe even get back to where you were.

GWEN
   Back to where we were?

KAREN
   I mean your life … the one you had.

GWEN
   Without you? Not a chance.

KAREN
   You know, most people move on from the bad things that happen to them. They get on with their lives.

GWEN
   Really? Why?

KAREN
   I don't know. That's just what they say.

GWEN
   Who? Who says that?

KAREN
   It's just … said.

GWEN
   Yeah well … getting on with your life in some fashion and going back to a life that's no longer there, two different things, right.

KAREN
>Yeah ... but moving out of here is a possibility? Getting some kind of income and—

GWEN
>You mean like that coffee cart idea?

KAREN
>Coffee cart? If that's enough for you. And then moving to someplace where you could have your own room ...

GWEN
>Privacy isn't such a big deal for us anymore ... But we could look into it, I guess. I mean your father would probably be up for that eventually.

KAREN
>Eventually.

GWEN
>Right now we're okay where we are, doing what we need to do. Your father's got his sloganizing, and since no one else is committed to keeping these shoes safe ... okay?

>*GWEN reaches out for KAREN's hand.*

KAREN
>Okay.

>*Blackout.*

Scene 22

NED on the street, on the lookout. VONNEGUT just watches.

VONNEGUT
You picked someone out yet?

NED
I'm narrowing it down.

VONNEGUT
There's a fairly good chance you'll choose someone relatively innocent.

NED
That's why I'm taking my time.

VONNEGUT
That won't necessarily help.

NED
I'd really appreciate it if you got on board with this.

VONNEGUT
No ... you want me to talk you out of it.

NED
It's not like I need to do it.

VONNEGUT
So don't.

NED
> The point I was trying to make is that it's not for me per se. It's for the overall good.

VONNEGUT
> Unless you kill some family's sole provider. Not much overall good in that.

NED
> They won't have a family.

VONNEGUT
> You planning on killing more than one?

NED
> Not tonight ...

VONNEGUT
> Then it's not *they* ... Using *they* just impersonalizes it for you. It's he or she. You going to kill a woman?

NED
> I don't kill women.

VONNEGUT
> You've killed before?

NED
> No I mean when I do it ... when I see who it is who has to have it done to them, I know it won't be a woman. There are too many men who deserve it more.

VONNEGUT
> What kind of men?

NED
> The harmful kind ...

VONNEGUT
> The harmful kind ... without a family?

NED
> I'll know if they have a family. I can tell. I had a family. I know what I looked like—

VONNEGUT
> When you had a family, an intact family, before your son just pissed off, your daughter got killed. You think you looked the same after all that? You think you might wind up killing a man who looks like you looked then ... just haunted, just in pain ... alone in his pain.

NED
> People need to be removed from our midst. There are some very bad people who need to be taken out of the picture.

VONNEGUT
> Maybe you could just send them all to one of those other dimensions you've been thinking so much about.

NED
> Don't think I haven't considered it. (*looks at him*) You like that idea?

VONNEGUT
> Well I think you got it from me, so yeah. But we're not even close to realizing how to do that so—

NED
> No I wouldn't get my hopes up or anything. But just thinking that eventually there's going to be another way to deal with all the selfish deadly crappy people in the world—

VONNEGUT
    Might be enough to stop you from going on a killing spree?

NED
    I'm just saying I have to believe that something will eventually get done ... to stop people from hurting all the people like us who can't stand being hurt much longer. I really need to believe that will happen one day. I'm not kidding. This no fucking joke.

VONNEGUT
    Got it.

NED
    I mean it.

VONNEGUT
    I know. Relax.

NED
    Relax ...

        Blackout.

Scene 23

> *NED and GWEN on the street with a stolen hospital cart on which sits a large stolen coffee urn, some stolen cups and a tray of lemon tarts. VONNEGUT watches from a distance.*

NED
 Fresh coffee!

GWEN
 Free coffee! Brewed not perked!

NED
 As if they care ...

GWEN
 It's better.

NED
 As if they care if it's better.

GWEN
 They'll learn to care.

NED
 Sorry. It's not a part of their culture. Caring ... about anything ...

GWEN
 I don't think that's true.

NED
> Guy in the shelter last night, standing there, arm dangling at his side. Other guy asks him what's wrong, first guy says, "Broke my arm ... spits on the floor, then adds, "Not that I give a fuck"

GWEN
> So they'll learn to give a fuck. They'll learn lots of things. I'll teach them Latin.

NED
> Latin? Jesus. Why Latin. Why not mountain climbing ... Better you teach them how to sew.

GWEN
> Well first someone would have to teach *me* ... You could help them learn to manage their finances.

NED
> If they had finances ...

GWEN
> Well you could teach them how to *get* finances.

NED
> They'll never get finances. That's too much of a leap.

GWEN
> The future is only possible if we make a leap.

NED
> Vonnegut say that?

GWEN
> No, me ...

NED
> Well he probably said something like that.

GWEN
>   Yeah probably. But better. More elegant ...

NED
>   I'm just saying ... he's Vonnegut.

GWEN
>   And I'm not.

NED
>   I'm planning to talk to him about some of these other dimensions I'm on to.

GWEN
>   When you say on to ... ?

NED
>   That I suspect exist.

GWEN
>   Because?

NED
>   Because I've had time to consider the prospect. And why wouldn't they? Why would it just be this?

GWEN
>   Why wouldn't it just be this?

NED
>   I'm not actually prepared to debate it yet. That's why I need to talk to Vonnegut some more. I need more information.

GWEN
>   You think he has information about other dimensions?

NED
> Well I know it's one of the things he's thought about.
>> *GWEN looks at him, smiles, then turns out.*

GWEN
> Fresh coffee!

NED
> And lemon tarts!

GWEN
> Lemon tarts made by *him*!

NED
> Like they care who made them ...

GWEN
> I'm sure they will when they find out how hard it was. Steal the flour, steal the sugar, the lemons ... steal this cart.

NED
> They steal things all the time. That's no big deal.

GWEN
> It is for us.

NED
> Well actually ... no it's not.

GWEN
> Yeah ... you're right. How about that for a dramatic change ... (*looks around*) Why aren't they coming to get any? ... (*appealing to passersby*) Fresh brewed coffee! Tasty lemon tarts!

NED
> They're suspicious. They're probably asking themselves what we want in return. Do we want them to volunteer some time, give blood, turn to Jesus ...

GWEN
> (*to anyone*) We don't want anything! Not a thing! Honest!

NED
> Well we want to feel good about doing this. We're still middle class at heart.

GWEN
> I stopped being middle class when Karen got that disease. From then on I was the mother of a paranoid bipolar, schizophrenic and nothing else ... And anyway, even if they don't want anything from us, I feel good just for making the effort.

NED
> Well then you're more evolved than I am. Because we put a lot of work into helping those wretched fuckers.

GWEN
> Where's your gun?

NED
> Sorry?

GWEN
> Your gun. You still have it?

NED
> No ... no I got rid of it.

GWEN
: Really. So you've decided we're going to live then. You're not going to kill us both one night while I'm sleeping.

NED
: No ... not for now, anyway.

GWEN
: I'm okay with that.

NED
: Good ...

Blackout.

End.